The dates of Haggai's messages have been converted by Bible scholars and historians to correspond to modern calendars. They remind us that Haggai was a real person who really spoke these words to God's people on these specific days.

Haggai's feast

John Brown
Brian Wright

CF4·K

Haggai's name means **"feast,"**
but the feasts weren't very festive in Haggai's day.

You see, Israel had stopped building **God's temple.**

So God stopped the **rain,**

which stopped the **crops,**

which left the people **hungry,**

and **thirsty.**

So God sent his prophet Haggai to tell
his people to **get busy building** his temple.

Why did God's temple need rebuilding? Because Israel had been **very bad** for a **very long time.**

So God sent a wicked nation to knock down
his temple and take the Israelites **far, far away.**

But God is very good and very forgiving, so after
a long time, he brought his people **home again.**

When they got home, God told them, "Rebuild my temple
first, then you can work on your own houses and farms."

So they did ... for a while.

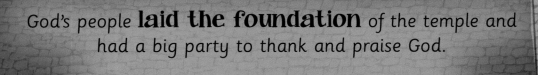

God's people **laid the foundation** of the temple and had a big party to thank and praise God.

BUT some of their neighbors didn't like God and told them to **stop building,** or else!

Then God's enemies told lies to the authorities, who told them to **stop, or else!**

So Israel disobeyed God and **stopped rebuilding** his temple like he told them.

Instead, they **built fancy homes** for themselves and started farming their own land. They forgot about God and **did what they wanted**, which was a really, really bad idea.

And so ...

They planted **much**
but harvested **little.**

They drank **a lot**
but stayed **thirsty.**

They dressed **warm**,
but stayed **cold.**

They worked **hard**
but had **no money.**

Then the rain **stopped**
and the crops **died**.

God was teaching them a lesson.

"Disobeying me is always a really, really **bad idea."**

That's when God sent Haggai to deliver
five messages on **four days.**

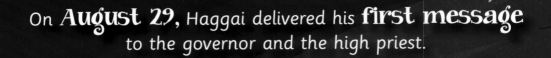

On **August 29**, Haggai delivered his **first message** to the governor and the high priest.

"God says,
'Tell my people to **get back to work** rebuilding my temple!'"

So God's children started building again, and God started blessing them again. God was teaching his children that we can only be **happy** when we **obey** him.

Haggai's **second message** came on **September 21**
during Israel's autumn harvest feast.

"'I am with you,' says the Lord!"

This made everyone so happy that they
finished the temple in less than a month!

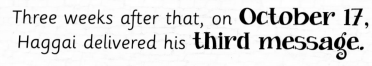

Three weeks after that, on **October 17,**
Haggai delivered his **third message.**

"Who remembers the first temple before it got
knocked down? It was bigger and better
than this new one, wasn't it?"

"But don't be sad; **be strong!**
Someday God will live in this temple and make
everything wonderful everywhere!"

Haggai delivered his **last two messages** on **December 18.**

"If your hands are dirty, anything you touch gets dirty, right? Well, you've made everything dirty by disobeying me. This is why you never had enough food, water, money, or warmth.

But now that you've started obeying me again,
I will bless you."

Haggai's **last message** was the best of all.

"Someday I will get rid of your enemies and establish my **Forever King.** I, the Lord of the angel armies, have spoken!"

When Haggai got to **heaven,**
he learned **something special** you may already know...

This Forever King is none other than God's own Son,

Jesus Christ!

The King came to earth at **Christmas**, died on **Good Friday,** and came back to life on **Easter** so that we could live with God in heaven, too.

All we have to do is be truly sorry for our sins
and trust in Jesus alone to save us.
This can be done by a prayer like this,
if you really mean it!

"God, I've done bad things, and I'm sorry.

I believe that Jesus is your Son,

and that he died for me on the cross.

So please forgive me and

let me serve King Jesus from now on.

Amen."

Although Haggai delivered his **five messages** long ago,
they still apply to us today.

Don't disobey God,
for he disciplines
the disobedient.

Be brave,
for God is with us.

Stand strong,
for God is coming.

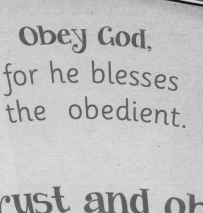

Obey God,
for he blesses
the obedient.

Trust and obey
King Jesus,

for he is God's

Forever King!

Christian Focus Publications publishes books for adults and children under its four main imprints: Christian Focus, CF4K, Mentor and Christian Heritage. Our books reflect our conviction that God's Word is reliable and Jesus is the way to know him, and live for ever with him.

Our children's publication list covers pre-school to early teens. We also publish personal and family devotional titles, biographies and inspirational stories that children will love.

From pre-school board books to teenage apologetics, we have it covered!

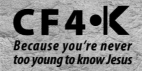

CF4•K
Because you're never
too young to know Jesus